T4-ABJ-061

Splash and Flow

Splash and Flow

text by Ruth Howell
photographs by Arline Strong

Atheneum 1973 New York

For Joshua, Julie and Ann

Copyright © 1973 by Ruth Howell
Photographs copyright © 1973 by Arline Strong
All rights reserved
Library of Congress catalog card number 72-86949
ISBN 0-689-30101-4
Published simultaneously in Canada by
McClelland & Stewart, Ltd.
Manufactured in the United States of America
Printed by Connecticut Printers, Inc., Hartford
Bound by A. Horowitz & Son/Bookbinders
Clifton, New Jersey
First Edition

Splash and Flow

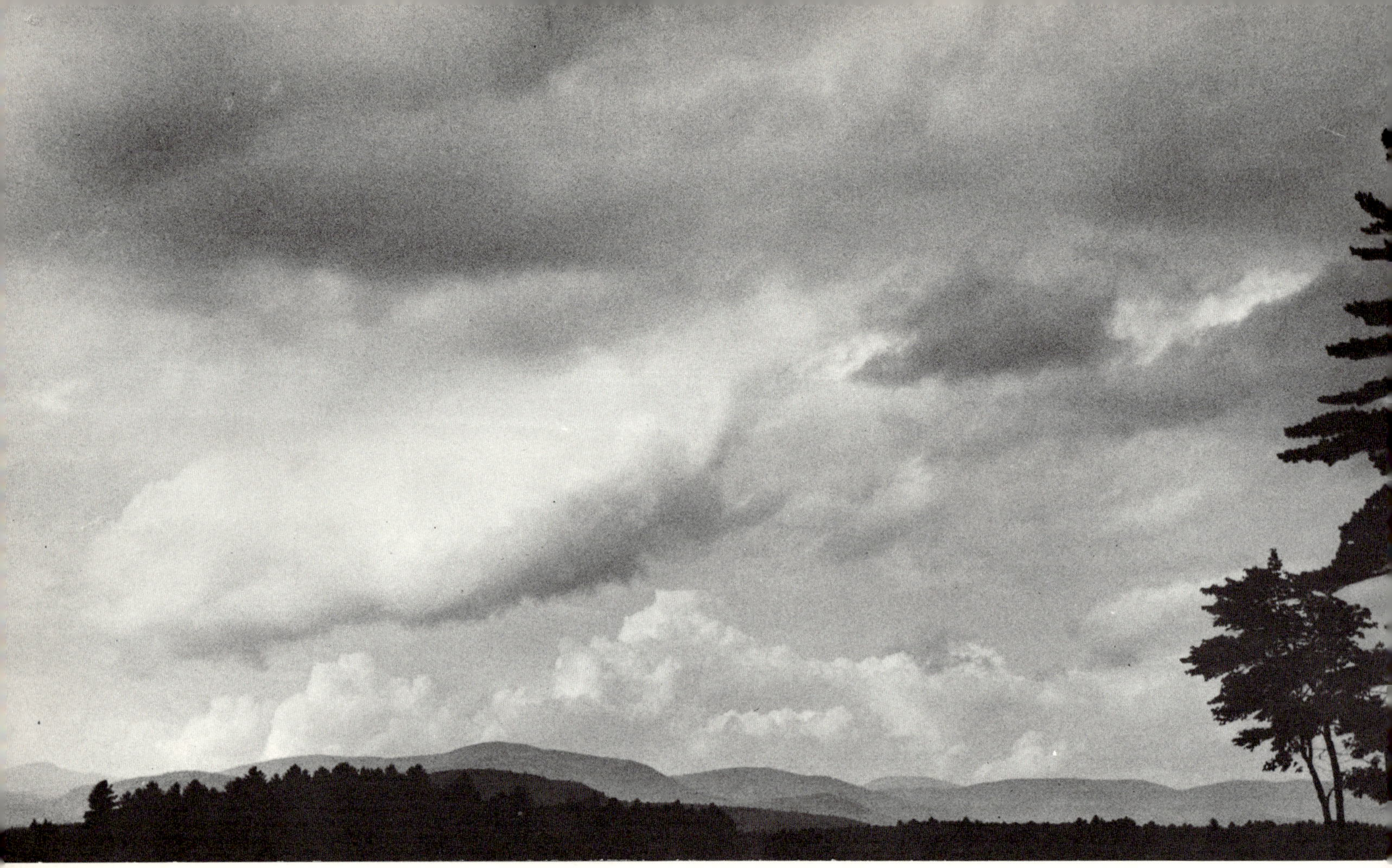

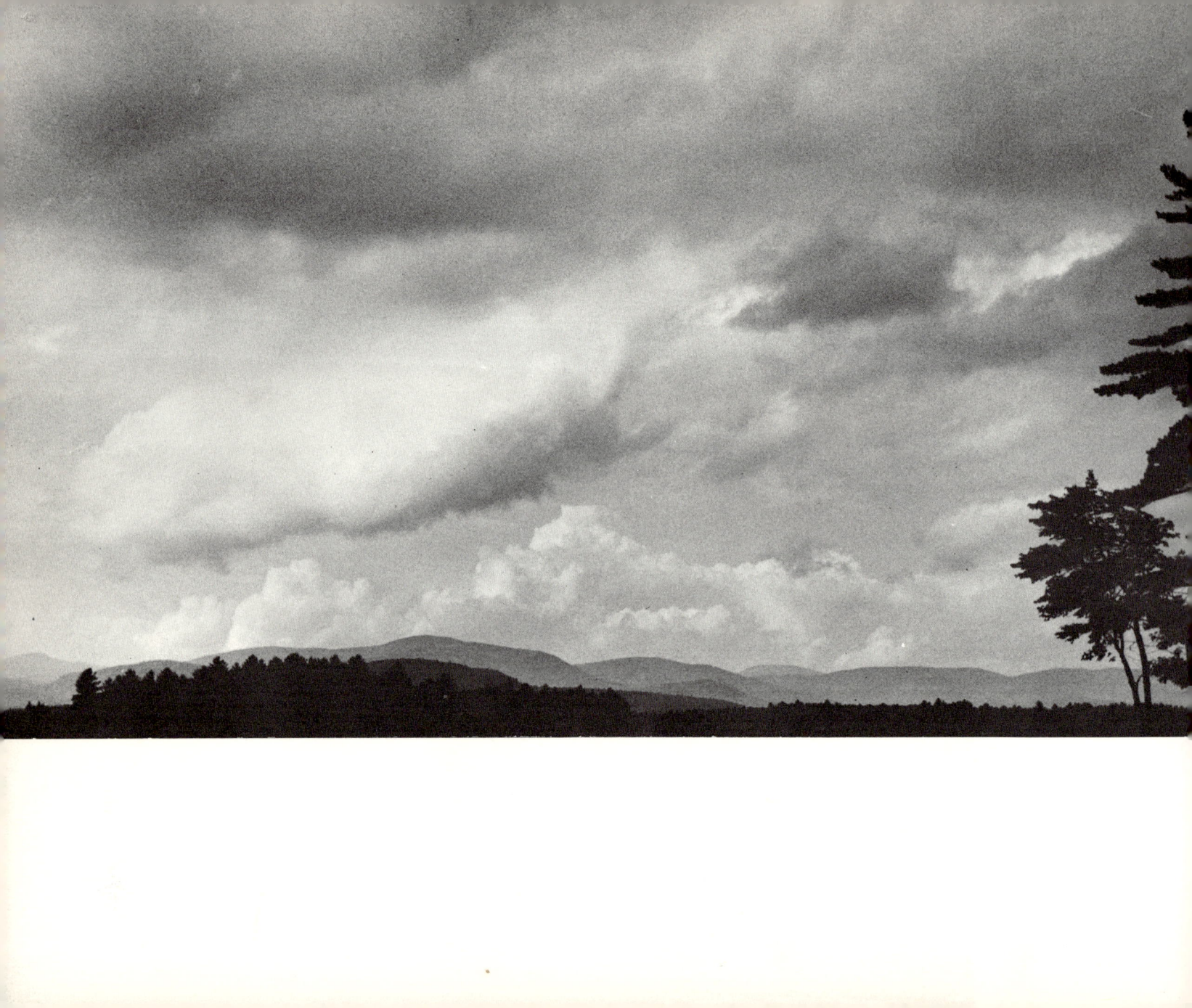

All over the land, whenever gray clouds cover the sky,
people say to each other, "It's going to rain soon."

When it rains put on your boots,
and put up your umbrella.
Listen to the raindrops tapping there above you.

But suppose it never rained.
You couldn't keep a turtle
or an angelfish for a pet.

And you could never visit
the seals at the zoo.

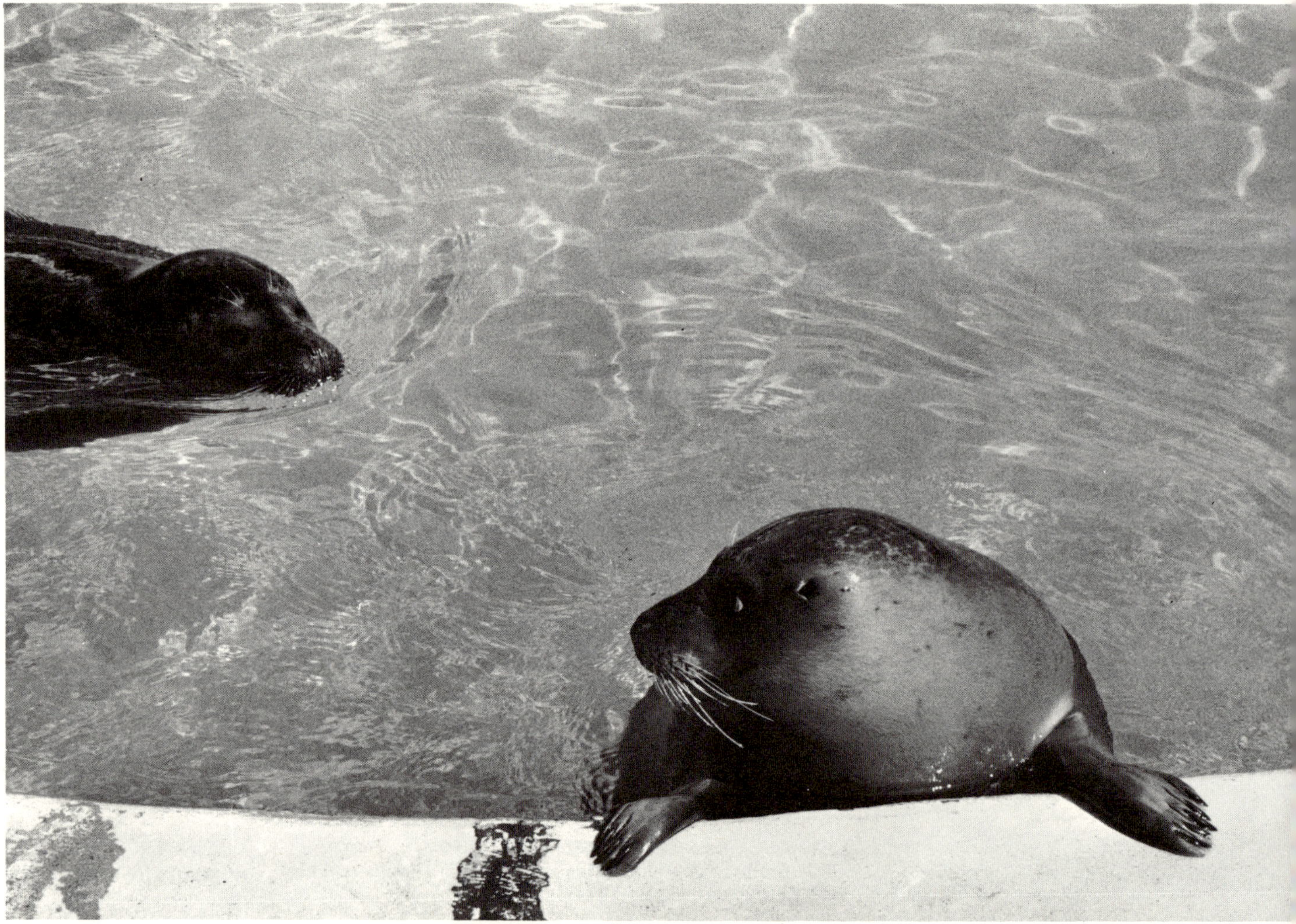

There would be no ponds—no homes for frogs.

And if it never rained, there would be no puddles
for you to splash in or to look for reflections.

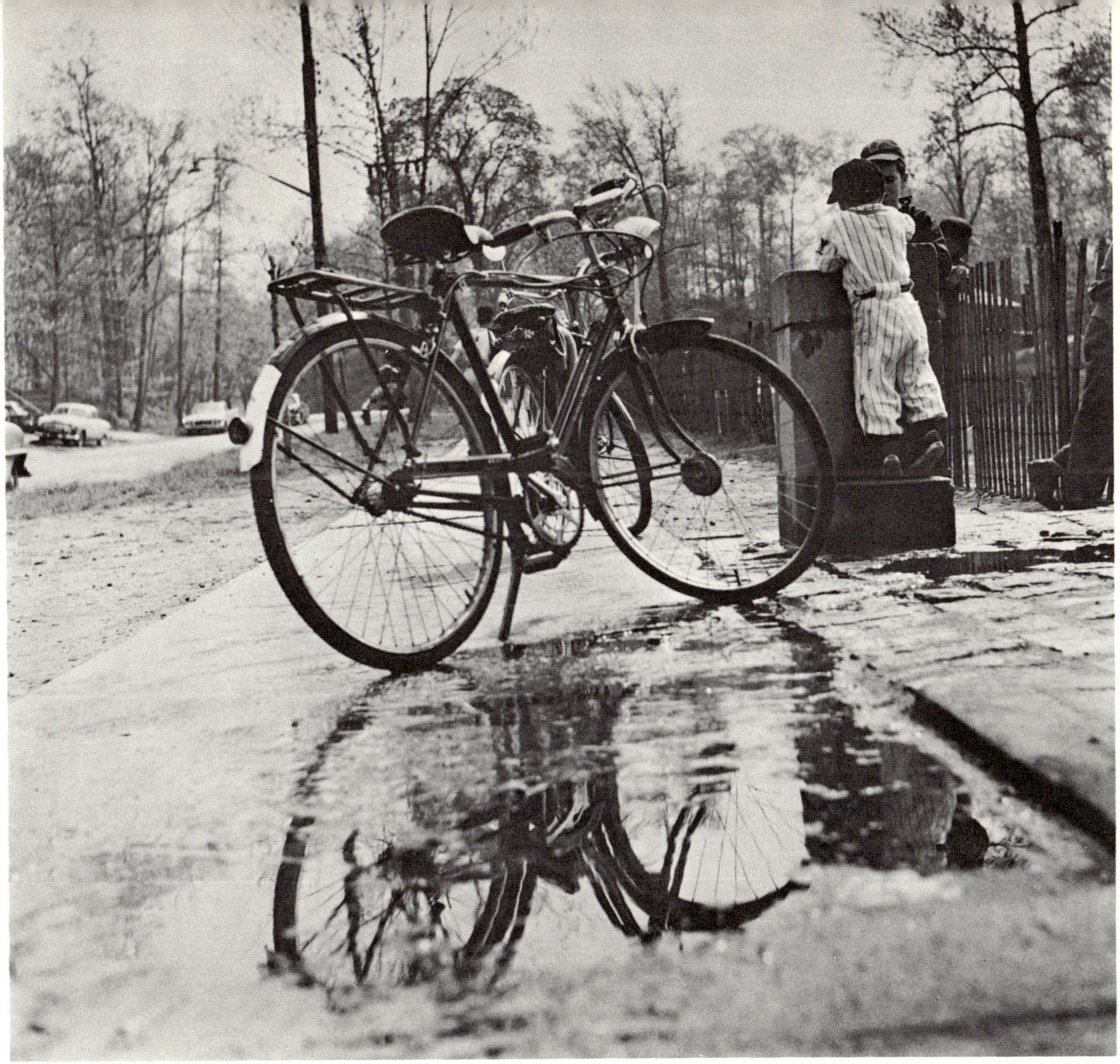

If it never rained,
there would be no wide rivers
flowing to the oceans,

which are the widest waters of all.

Boats couldn't
float without water,

and neither could ducks

or rafts.

You couldn't run under a sprinkler,

and neither could a puppy.

In winter you'd never find transparent icicles.

We all need water. We need it for washing,

and we need it for cooking. When you cook chestnuts,
the water and the nuts get hotter,
and the nuts change from hard to soft.
But what happens to eggs if you boil them in water?

You use water to soften clay,
so you can push it into any shape you like.

You use water to mix with paint,

and you use it for soap bubbles,

and discovering what floats and what sinks.

Firemen need water to put out dangerous fires,
and you need it too—to quench your fire after a cookout.

Whenever you turn on a faucet, water runs out.
Once that water was rain.
A raindrop changes
its shape over and over again before it flows
from your faucet.

When rain falls on mountain forests,
and when snow melts there in springtime,
all that water disappears into the ground
very quickly, for forest ground is like
a great big sponge. But soon some of
the water trickles out of the ground
again and makes streams and ponds.

People who live near mountain forests
can get all the water they need
from a pond or a stream nearby.

But water for city people
has to travel a long, long way.
As one tiny brook tumbles
down the mountain, other brooks
join it, until at last they
become a wide river. You can
make brooks and rivers, too,
when you play in the sand.

When the men who are in charge of water for the city get ready to make water flow from thousands and thousands of city faucets, they first build a wall called a dam across a river. Behind that dam the river water spreads out and makes a lake called a reservoir.

If you go to the country in the summer, you may find a brook. Then build a dam of your own of leaves and stones and sticky mud.

Water for the city runs out of the reservoir through a tunnel deep under the ground. When that water reaches the city, it is divided into pipes called water mains. There is a water main pipe under every street, and you may be able to find where they are. Look for big iron lids in the street near corners. Some of these cover water mains. The lids are called manhole covers, because if a main pipe starts to leak, a man can take the cover off, and reach down to turn a valve with a long pole. A valve is like the handle of a water faucet only five times bigger. When the man turns the valve, no more water can move through the main pipe, and all the people who live on that street must manage without water until he has repaired the leak.

From the water mains, pipes branch out in every direction to take water to every building

and every fire hydrant in town.

Water works for people all the time.
It makes highways for tugboats.

If you make a little paddle-wheel boat,
the paddle will spin and push against
the water around it, and that pushing will
send your boat whizzing—full speed ahead.

Water cannot go uphill by itself, but it goes downhill with a rush and a roar.

A small waterfall will push a small wheel around,
and some big waterfalls are so powerful that
they turn the big wheels that make electricity.

Water can work and water can play.
Waves will chase you up a sandy beach.

Fountains play tricks. when you watch you can't always be sure how high they will leap.

Raindrops dance on a branch after a shower.

Snowflakes swoop and swirl
and tickle your face,
before they settle down
and make a soft white
blanket over the ground.

But best of all you can play with water. Fish in it.

Squirt it.

Skate on it when it freezes.

And make mud pies.

Then when you get thirsty, take a long cold drink.

Trees and flowers and animals and insects
and fish and reptiles all drink water too.

Water helps them grow bigger and stronger just like you.